I0103619

C. M. Badger, Elisabeth Woodburn

Floral Belles from the Green-house and Garden

C. M. Badger, Elisabeth Woodburn

Floral Belles from the Green-house and Garden

ISBN/EAN: 9783337272142

Printed in Europe, USA, Canada, Australia, Japan

Cover: Foto ©Andreas Hilbeck / pixelio.de

More available books at **www.hansebooks.com**

FLORAL BELLES

GREEN-HOUSE AND GARDEN.

PAINTED FROM NATURE,

BY

MRS. C. M. BADGER.

AUTHOR OF "WILD FLOWERS."

"BEAUTIFUL FLOWERS, WHOSE TENDER FORMS
SURVIVE THE DEADLY LIGHTNING'S GLARE,
AND BEND YOUR BOSOMS TO THE STORMS
THAT RIDE UPON THE MIDNIGHT AIR;

SAY, WERE YE ONLY BORN TO FADE?
OR WERE YOUR TINTS AND ODORS GIVEN
TO GRANT THE SPIRIT, IN THE SHADE
OF THIS DULL WORLD, SOME GLIMPSE OF HEAVEN?"

W. MARTIN.

NEW YORK:
CHARLES SCRIBNER & COMPANY, 654 BROADWAY.
1867.

JOHN F. TROW & CO.,
Printers, Stereotypers, and Electrotypers,
50 Greene Street.

LIST OF FLOWERS.

POETRY.

FLOWERS.

Spake full well, in language quaint and olden,
  One who dwelleth by the castled Rhine,
When he called the flowers so blue and golden,
  Stars, that in earth's firmament do shine.

Stars they are, wherein we read our history,
  As astrologers and seers of old;
Yet not wrapped about with awful mystery,
  Like the burning stars which they beheld.

Wondrous truths, and manifold as wondrous,
  God hath written in those stars above;
But not less in the bright flowrets under us,
  Stands the revelation of his love.

Bright and glorious is that revelation,
  Written all over this bright world of ours;
Making evident our own creation,
  In these stars of earth,—these golden flowers.

And the Poet, faithful and far-seeing,
  Sees alike in stars and flowers a part
Of the self-same, universal being,
  Which is throbbing in his brain and heart.

Gorgeous flowrets in the sunlight shining,
  Blossoms flaunting in the eye of day,
Tremulous leaves, with soft and silver lining,
  Buds that open only to decay.

Brilliant hopes, all woven in gorgeous tissues,
  Flaunting gaily in the golden light;
Large desires, with most uncertain issues,
  Tender wishes, blossoming at night!

FLOWERS.

These in flowers and men are more than seeming;
  Workings are they of the self-same powers,
Which the Poet, in no idle dreaming,
  Seeth in himself and in the flowers.

Everywhere about us are they glowing,
  Some like stars, to tell us Spring is born;
Others, their blue eyes with tears o'erflowing,
  Stand like Ruth amid the golden corn;

Not alone in Spring's armorial bearing,
  And in Summer's green emblazon'd field,
But in arms of brave old Autumn's wearing.
  In the centre of his brazen shield;

Not alone in meadows and green alleys,
  On the mountain-top and by the brink
Of sequestered pools in woodland valleys,
  Where the slaves of nature stoop to drink;

Not alone in her vast dome of glory,
  Not on graves of bird and beast alone,
But in old cathedrals high and hoary,
  On the tombs of heroes, carved in stone;

In the cottage of the rudest peasant,
  In ancestral homes, whose crumbling towers
Speaking of the Past unto the Present,
  Tell us of the ancient Games of Flowers;

In all places, then, and in all seasons,
  Flowers expand their light and soul-like wings,
Teaching us, by most persuasive reasons,
  How akin they are to human things.

And with child-like, credulous affection
  We behold their tender buds expand;
Emblems of our own great resurrection,
  Emblems of the bright and better land.

LONGFELLOW.

THE CAMELLIA JAPONICA.

As Venus wandered midst the Italian bower,
  And marked the loves and graces round her play;
  She plucked a *musk-rose* from its dew-bent spray,
"And this," she cried, "shall be my favorite flower;
For o'er its crimson leaflets I will shower
  Dissolving sweets to steal the soul away;
  That Dian's self shall own their sovereign sway,
And feel the influence of my mightier power!"
Then spoke fair Cynthia, as severe she smiled,—
"Be others by thy amorous arts beguiled;
  Ne'er shall thy dangerous gifts these brows adorn;
To me more dear than all their rich perfume
The chaste Camellia's pure and spotless bloom,
  That boasts no fragrance, and conceals no thorn."

WILLIAM ROSCOE.

NIGHT-SCENTED FLOWERS.

Call back your odors, lovely flowers,
  From the night-winds, call them back;
And fold your leaves till the laughing hours
  Come forth in the sunbeam's track.

The lark lies couched in his grassy nest,
  And the honey-bee is gone;
And all bright things are away to rest,
  Why watch ye here alone?

"Nay, let our shadowy beauty bloom,
  When the stars give quiet light;
And let us offer our faint perfume
  On the silent shrine of night.

"Call it not wasted, the scent we lend
  To the breeze, when no step is nigh;
Oh, thus forever the earth should send
  Her grateful breath on high!

"And love us as emblems, night's dewy flowers,
  Of hopes unto sorrows given,
That spring through the gloom of the darkest hours,
  Looking alone to heaven."

MRS. HEMANS.

BRING FLOWERS.

Bring flowers, young flowers, for the festal board,
To wreathe the cup ere the wine is pour'd;
Bring flowers! they are springing in wood and vale,
Their breath floats out on the southern gale,
And the touch of the sunbeam hath waked the rose,
To deck the hall where the bright wine flows.

Bring flowers to strew in the conqueror's path —
He hath shaken thrones with his stormy wrath!
He comes with the spoils of the nations back,
The vines lie crushed in his chariot's track,
The turf looks red where he won the day —
Bring flowers to die in the conqueror's way!

Bring flowers to the captive's lonely cell,
They have tales of the joyous woods to tell;
Of the free blue streams, and the glowing sky,
And the bright world shut from his languid eye;
They will bear him a thought of the sunny hours,
And a dream of his youth — bring him flowers, wild flowers.

Bring flowers, fresh flowers, for the bride to wear;
They were born to blush in her shining hair.
She is leaving the home of her childhood's mirth,
She hath bid farewell to her father's hearth,
Her place is now by another's side —
Bring flowers for the locks of the fair young bride.

Bring flowers, pale flowers, o'er the bier to shed,
A crown for the brow of the early dead!
For this through its leaves hath the white rose burst,
For this in the woods was the violet nursed.
Though they smile in vain for what once was ours,
They are love's last gift — bring ye flowers, pale flowers!

Bring flowers to the shrine where we kneel in prayer,
They are nature's offering, their place is *there!*
They speak of hope to the fainting heart,
With a voice of promise, they come and part,
They sleep in dust through the wintry hours,
They break forth in glory — bring flowers, bright flowers.

MRS. HEMANS

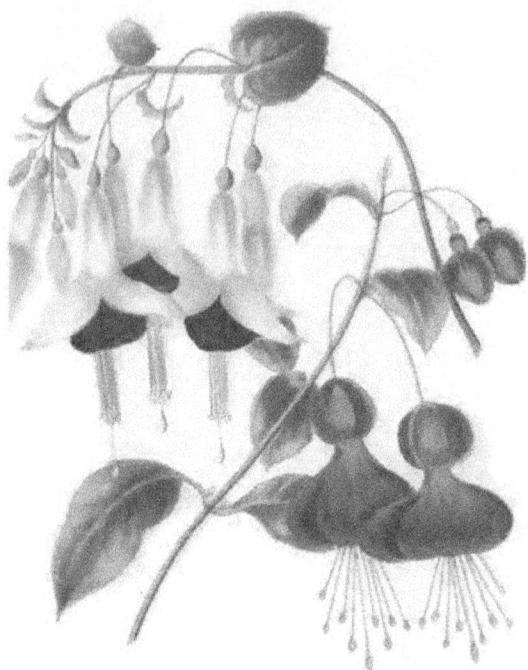

TO THE CACTUS SPECIOSISSIMUS.

Who hung thy beauty on such rugged stalk,
Thou glorious flower?
                    Who poured the richest hues,
In varying radiance, o'er thine ample brow,
And like a mesh, those tissued stamens laid
Upon thy crimson lip?
                    Thou glorious flower!
Methinks it were no sin to worship thee,
Such passport hast thou from thy Maker's hand
To thrill the soul. Lone, on thy leafless stem,
Thou bidd'st the queenly rose, with all her buds,
Do homage, and the greenhouse peerage bow
Their rainbow coronets.
                    Hast thou no thought?
No intellectual life? thou who canst wake
Man's heart to such communings? no sweet word
With which to answer him? 'T would almost seem
That so much beauty needs must have a soul,
And that such form as tints the gazer's dream,
Held higher spirit than the common clod
On which we tread.
                    Yet while we muse, a blight
Steals o'er thee, and thy shrinking bosom shows
The mournful symptoms of a wan disease.—
I will not stay to see thy beauty fade.
——Still must I bear away within my heart
Thy lesson of our own mortality;
The fearful witherings of each blossomed bough
On which we lean, of every bud we fain
Would hide within our bosoms from the touch
Of the destroyer.
                    So instruct us, Lord!
Thou Father of the sunbeam and the soul,
Even by the simple sermon of a flower,
To cling to Thee.

                              MRS. SIGOURNEY.

26.

THE CHILD AND FLOWERS.

Hast thou been in the woods with the honey-bee ?
Hast thou been with the lamb in the pastures free ?
With the hare through the copses and dingles wild ?
With the butterfly over the heath, fair child ?
Yes ; the light fall of thy bounding feet
Hath not startled the wren from her mossy seat ;
Yet hast thou ranged the green forest dells,
And brought back a treasure of buds and bells.

Thou know'st not the sweetness, by antique song,
Breathed o'er the names of that flowery throng ;
The woodbine, the primrose, the violet dim,
The lily that gleams by the fountain's brim ;
These are old words, that have made each grove
A dreamy haunt for romance and love ;
Each sunny bank, where faint odors lie,
A place for the gushings of poesy.

Thou know'st not the light wherewith fairy lore
Sprinkles the turf and the daisies o'er ;
Enough for thee are the dews that sleep,
Like hidden gems in the flower-urns deep ;
Enough the rich crimson spots that dwell
'Midst the gold of the cowslip's perfumed cell ;
And the scent by the blossoming sweetbriers shed,
And the beauty that bows the wood-hyacinth's head.

Oh ! happy child, in thy fawn-like glee,
What is remembrance or thought to thee ?
Fill thy bright locks with those gifts of Spring ;
O'er thy green pathway their colors fling ;
Bind them in chaplet and wild festoon —
What if to droop and to perish soon ?
Nature has mines of such wealth — and thou
Never wilt prize its delights as now.

THE CHILD AND FLOWERS.

For a day is coming to quell the tone
That rings in thy laughter, thou joyous one!
And to dim thy brow with a touch of care,
Under the gloss of its clustering hair;
And to tame the flash of thy cloudless eyes
Into the stillness of autumn skies;
And to teach thee that grief hath her needful part
'Midst the hidden things of each human heart.

Yet, shall we mourn, gentle child, for this?
Life hath enough of yet holier bliss.
Such be thy portion! the bliss to look
With a reverent spirit through Nature's book;
By fount, by forest, by river's line,
To track the paths of a love divine;
To read its deep meaning — to see and hear
God in earth's garden, — and not to fear.

MRS. HEMANS

THE CONSTANT FRIENDS.

O sweet souled flowers with robes so bright,
　Fair guests of Eden-birth,
In changeful characters of light,
What lines of love divine ye write
　Upon this troubled earth!

Man sinn'd in Paradise, and fell —
　But when the storm arose -
When thorns and brambles sow'd his path,
And gentlest natures turned to wrath,
　Ye leagued not with his foes.

Ye sinn'd not, though to him ye clung,
　When, at the guarded door,
The penal sword its terrors flung,
And warn'd him, with its flaming tongue,
　To enter there no more.

Forth by his side ye meekly far'd,
　With pure, reproachless eye,
And when the vengeful lion roar'd,
A balmy gush of fragrance pour'd,
　In hallow'd sympathy.

Ye sprang amid the broken sod,
　His weary brow to kiss;
Bloom'd at his feet where'er he trod,
And told his burden'd heart of God,
　And of a world of bliss.

Ye bow'd the head to teach him how
　He must himself decay:
Yet, dying, charged each tiny seed
The earliest call of Spring to heed,
　And cheer his future way.

From age to age, with dewy sigh,
　Even from the desert glade,
Sweet words ye whisper, till ye die
Still pointing to that cloudless sky,
　Where beauty cannot fade.

Mrs. Sigourney.

THE WINGED PASSION-FLOWER.

Beneath the covert of o'erarching trees
Bright *Maracuia* [a] woos the cooling breeze,
The passing Indian turns the admiring eye,
Smit by the glories of her crimson dye,
And stops in pleas'd attention, to survey
Her vivid leaves and variegated ray.—
But loftier thoughts the rising mind inspire
When warm devotion leads her holy fire.
Haply amid the convent's virgin train,
Bosom'd in shades beyond the western main,
At rosy morn, or evening's silent hour,
Some fair enthusiast views the sainted flower :
When, lo ! to rapt imagination's eye
Springs the sad scene of darken'd Calvary !
The thorny crown the heavenly brows around,
The scourging thongs, the galling cords that bound,
And nails that pierced with agonizing wound.
Sudden she lifts to heaven her ardent eye
In silent gaze and solemn ecstacy ;
Then, filled with timid hope and holy fear,
Drops on the flower a consecrated tear.

SHAW.

* The ancient American name of the flower.

THE LANGUAGE OF FLOWERS.

In Eastern lands they talk in flowers,
  And tell in a garland their loves and cares ;
Each blossom that blooms in their garden bowers,
  On its leaves a mystic language bears.

The rose is a sign of joy and love,
  Young blushing love in its earliest dawn ;
And the mildness that suits the gentle dove,
  From the myrtle's snowy flower is drawn.

Innocence shines in the lily's bell,
  Pure as a heart in its native heaven ;
Fame's bright star, and glory's swell,
  By the glossy leaf of the bay are given.

The silent, soft, and humble heart
  In the violet's hidden sweetness breathes ;
And the tender soul that cannot part,
  A twine of evergreen fondly wreathes.

The cypress that darkly shades the grave,
  Is sorrow that mourns her bitter lot ;
And faith that a thousand ills can brave,
  Speaks in thy blue leaves, forget-me-not.

Then gather a wreath from the garden bowers,
And tell the wish of thy heart in flowers.

PERCIVAL.

A WILD OF FLOWERS.

A Tulip blossomed one morning in May,
    By the side of a sanded alley ;
Its leaves were dressed in a rich array,
Like the clouds at the earliest dawn of day,
    When the mist rolls over the valley ;
The dew had descended the night before,
    And lay in its velvet bosom,
And its spreading urn was flowing o'er,
And the crystal heightened the tints it bore
    On its yellow and crimson blossom.

A sweet Red-rose, on its bending thorn,
    Its bud was newly spreading,
And the flowing effulgence of early morn
    Its beams on its breast was shedding ;
The petals were heavy with dripping tears,
    That twinkled in pearly brightness,
And the thrush in its covert thrilled my ears
    With a varied song of lightness.

A Lily, in mantle of purest snow,
    Hung over a silent fountain,
And the wave in its calm and quiet flow,
Displayed its silken leaves below,
    Like the drift on the windy mountain ;
It bowed with the moisture, the night had wept,
    When the stars shone over the billow,
And white-winged spirits their vigils kept,
Where beauty and innocence sweetly slept
    On its pure and thornless pillow.

A Hyacinth lifted its purple bell
    From the slender leaves around it ;
It curved its cup in a flowing swell,
    And a starry circle crowned it ;
The deep-blue tincture, that robed it, seemed
    The gloomiest garb of sorrow,
As if on its eye no brightness beamed,
And it never in clearer moments dreamed
    Of a fair and a calm to-morrow.

A WILD OF FLOWERS.

A Daisy peeped from the tufted sod,
  In its bashful modesty drooping,
Where often the morn, as I lightly trod,
In bounding youth, the fallow clod,
  Had over it seen me stooping :
It looked in my face with a dewy eye
  From its ring of ruby lashes,
And it seemed, that a brighter was lurking by,
The fires of whose ebony lustre fly,
  Like summer's dazzling flashes.

And the wind, with a soft and silent wing,
  Brushed over this wild of flowers,
And it wakened the birds, who began to sing
Their hymn to the season of love and Spring,
  In the shade of the bending bowers ;
And it culled their full nectareous store,
  In its lightly fluttering motion,
As when from Hybla's murmuring shore
The evening breeze from her thyme-beds bore
  Her sweetness over the ocean.

PERCIVAL.

LOVE-IN-IDLENESS.

In gardens oft a beauteous flower there grows,
   By vulgar eyes unnoticed and unseen ;
In sweet security it humbly blows,
   And rears its purple head to deck the green.

This flower, as Nature's poet sweetly sings,
   Was once milk-white, and Heart's-ease was its name,
Till wanton Cupid poised his roseate wings,
   A vestal's sacred bosom to inflame.

With treacherous aim the god his arrow drew,
   Which she with icy coldness did repel ;
Rebounding thence with feathery speed it flew,
   Till on this lovely flower, at last, it fell.

Heart's-ease no more the wandering shepherds found ;
   No more the nymphs its snowy form possess ;
Its white now changed to purple by Love's wound,
   Heart's-ease no more, — 't is Love-in-idleness.

MRS. SHERIDAN.

THE MOSS ROSE.

The Angel of the Flowers, one day,
Beneath a rose-tree sleeping lay ;—
That spirit to whom charge is given,
To bathe young buds in dews of heaven :
Awaking from his light repose,
The Angel whispered to the Rose : —
" O, fondest object of my care,
Still fairest found, where all is fair ;
For the sweet shade thou giv'st to me,
Ask what thou wilt, 't is granted thee ! "
" Then," said the Rose, with deepened glow,
" On me another grace bestow."
The spirit paused in silent thought ; —
What grace was there the flower had not ? —
'T was but a moment — o'er the Rose
A veil of moss, the Angel throws ;
And robed in nature's simplest weed,
Could there a flower that Rose exceed ?

FROM THE GERMAN.

THE TULIP ROOT.

In the bulb of the Tulip are to be found, by the aid of the microscope, in midwinter, in perfect form and symmetry, the leaves and flower which the coming Spring is to develope.

When o'er the cultured lawns and dreary wastes
Retiring Autumn flings her howling blasts,
Bends in tumultuous waves the struggling woods,
And show'rs their leafy honors on the floods,
In with'ring heaps collects the flowery spoil,
And each chill insect sinks beneath the soil:
Quick hears fair Tulipa the loud alarms,
And folds her *infant* closer in her arms;
Soft plays affection round her bosom's throne,
And guards its life, *forgetful of her own.*
So wings the wounded deer her headlong flight,
Pierced by some ambush'd archer of the night,
Shoots to the woodlands with her bounding fawn,
And drops of blood bedew the conscious lawn:
There, hid in shades, she shuns the cheerful day,
Hangs o'er her young, and weeps her life away.
So stood *Eliza* on the wood-crowned height,
O'er Minden's plains, spectatress of the fight;
Sought with bold eye, amid the bloody strife,
Her dearer self, the partner of her life;
From hill to hill, the rushing host pursued,
And viewed his banner, or believed she viewed;
Pleased with the distant roar, with quicker tread,
Fast by her hand, one lisping boy she led,
And one fair girl amid the loud alarm,
Slept on her kerchief, cradled by her arm;
While round her brows bright beams of honor dart,
And love's warm eddies circle round her heart.
Near and more near th' intrepid beauty press'd,
Saw through the driving smoke his dancing crest,
Heard the exulting shout, "they run! they run!"
"Great God!" she cried, "he's safe! the battle's won!"

THE TULIP ROOT.

A ball now hisses through the airy tides,
Some fury wing'd it, and some demon guides,
Parts the fine locks her graceful head that deck,
Wounds her fair ear, and sinks into her neck ;
The red stream issuing from her azure veins
Dyes her white veil, her ivory bosom stains.
"Ah me !" she cried, and, sinking on the ground,
Kiss'd her dear babes, regardless of the wound :
"Oh ! cease not yet to beat, thou vital urn,
"Wait, gushing life, oh ! wait my Love's return ;
"Oh ! spare, ye war-hounds, spare their tender age ;
"On me, on me," she cried, "exhaust your rage."
Hoarse barks the wolf, the vulture screams from far,
The angel Pity shuns the walks of war ;
Then with weak arms her weeping babes caressed,
And, sighing, hid *them* in her *blood-stain'd vest.*

DARWIN.

TO THE ROSE OF GETHSEMANE.

The rose from which this drawing was taken, was picked in the Garden of Gethsemane, pressed and dried, and after remaining in this state several years, presented to the author. On immersing it in water, the petals became softened, and were placed in their original position; those in the center retained their beautiful color, as here exhibited, and the fragrance was like that of a fresh-blown rose.

Fair Rose of Gethsemane! nursed by the sod,
Which drank the hot tears of the sad Son of God,
When o'er the Brook Kedron, His weary steps led,
And those whom He loved, all forsook Him and fled;
When Judas betrayed Him, and Peter denied
The belov'd of His Father, God crucified.

Beholding, I wonder, thou beautiful thing,
Such fragrance and loveliness ever could spring
From that cold dewy garden, trampled and wet
With soldiers' rude feet and Christ's agonized sweat,
Which like drops of blood trickled down to the ground,
While timid disciples lay sleeping around.

And much do I wonder that in his distress,
His lips move to curse not, but only to bless:
That beauty still thrives, where such agony knelt,
From ground that had witnessed the sorrow he felt.
Though the fig-tree he cursed, he prayed for his foes,
And where thorns grew for Him, for them blooms the rose.

I look at thee weeping, thou innocent flower,
Fair silent memento of that dreadful hour.
He saw with a sorrow God only could feel,
The rabble blasphemers in mockery kneel;
His weeping eye saw what no mortal could see,
His own wounded side, on that ignoble tree.

62

TO THE ROSE OF GETHSEMANE.

I look at thee, smiling with joy through my tears,
Sweet Rose of Gethsemane, coffined for years :
My eager hand took thee, thy grave-clothes unbound,
When, lo ! in thy heart, a sweet perfume I found ;
And when from thy petals the bands were untied,
Like " Rose Damascena " thy fair cheek was dyed.

No more will I weep, then, thou child of a day ;
When ages have passed, in their swift course away,
Our Lord shall behold the redeem'd among men,
And all his soul's travail be satisfied then ;
With each ransomed soul, will the perfume remain,
Of those crimson drops from the Lamb that was slain.

C. M. B.

THE DEATH OF THE FLOWERS.

How happily, how happily, the flowers die away ;
Oh ! could we but return to earth as easily as they !
Just live a life of sunshine, of innocence, and bloom,
Then drop, without decrepitude or pain, into the tomb.

The gay and glorious creatures ! they neither " toil nor spin :"
Yet lo ! what goodly raiment they're all apparelled in :
No tears are on their beauty, but dewy gems more bright,
Than ever brow of eastern queen endiademed with light.

The young rejoicing creatures ! their pleasures never pall ;
Nor lose in sweet contentment, because so free to all !
The dew, the showers, the sunshine, the balmy blessed air,
Spend nothing of their freshness, though all may freely share.

The happy careless creatures ; of time they take no heed ;
Nor weary of his creeping, nor tremble at his speed ;
Nor sigh with sick impatience, and wish the light away ;
Nor when 'tis gone cry dolefully, " would God that it were day !"

And when their lives are over, they drop away to rest,
Unconscious of the penal doom, on holy Nature's breast ;
No pain have they in dying, no shrinking from decay :
Oh ! could we but return to earth as easily as they !

CAROLINE BOWLES.

FAREWELL TO THE FLOWERS.

Go to your peaceful rest,
  Friends of a brighter hour,
Jewels on youthful beauty's breast,
  Lights of the hall and bower ;
Well have ye done your part,
  Fair children of the sky,
We'll keep your memory in our heart,
  When low in dust ye lie.

Your gladness in our joy,
  Your smile beside our way,
Your gentle service round our bed
  Of sickness and decay,
Your rainbow on the cloud,
  Your sympathy in pain ;
We'll keep the memory of your deeds
  Until we meet again.

Rest from the blush of love ;
  Rest from the blight of care,
From the sweet nursing of your buds,
  And from the nipping air ;
Rest from the fever-thirst
  Of summer's noontide heat,
From coiling worm, and rifling hand,
  That vex'd your lone retreat.

If e'er ye thrilled with pride,
  When the admirer knelt,
Or on the lowly look'd with scorn,
  Which man for man hath felt ;
If through your bosoms pure
  Hath aught like evil flowed,
(Since folly may with angels dwell,)
  Rest from that painful load.

FAREWELL TO THE FLOWERS.

But not with grief or fear,
   Bow down the drooping head ;
See ! in the chamber of your birth
   Your dying couch is spread ;
Go ! strong in faith, ye flowers ;
   Strong in your guileless trust,
With the returning birds, to rise
   Above imprisoning dust.

Hear we a whisper low,
   From withering leaf and bell ?
" Our life hath been a dream of love,
   In garden or in dell ;
Yet wintry sleep we hail,
   And till the trump shall swell,
To wake us on the vernal morn,
   Sweet friends, a sweet farewell !"

MRS. SIGOURNEY.

www.ingramcontent.com/pod-product-compliance
Lightning Source LLC
Chambersburg PA
CBHW021626270326
41931CB00008B/894